Soul

Meets

Body

By

Jocelyn Mosman

Soul Meets Body

Jocelyn Mosman

Copyright © 2015

Jocelyn Mosman

jmosman7@aol.com
www.facebook.com/JocelynMosman

Whisky & Beards Publishing

www.whiskyandbeards.co.uk

Dedication

Jim and Jennifer Mosman,
Jessica, Jon, and Taylor Grondin,

Jan and William Stein,
Ann and Ed Mosman,

Craig Nelson, Robert Shaw, and Jelene Ballard

Preface

Dear Readers,

This collection of poetry, *Soul Meets Body*, is the final installation of the Soul Series. Being as such, this is the volume that allowed me to transition from what it meant to be a teenager to what it means to be a woman, emphasizing on my dreams, ambitions, and flaws.

As we travel together through the next 80 pages or so, I ask that you keep an open mind and an open heart. This is for the soul and for the body, for the beauty of each as they intermingle and weave their own elaborate stories and identities.

This book is told in 3 parts, and each is a stepping-stone in the journey toward acceptance. Please travel with me and learn to love the body and spirit you live in. Allow yourself the freedom to know and experience love.

Much love,
Jocelyn Mosman

Foreword

The journey of self-love is no small feat. The concept of a journey, in and of itself, necessitates an origin. For love to be the destination means that it must have been absent, twisted, confused, or denied to begin with. For love of one's self to be the arrival, it must also mean that a person's love has been directed elsewhere, whether the receiver deserved it, accepted it, and returned it or not.

The vulnerability of this journey is the power of Jocelyn Mosman's collection, *"Soul Meets Body."* Although each poem carries a distinct rhythm and microcosm of world building, the cumulative effect is one of sweet, then painful, and finally courageous discovery. Each moment unfolds like an unraveling tapestry of drama, with some threads returning, like the unnamed focus of the speaker's affection and, eventually, pain. And, as in effective drama, the speaker must come to terms with that pain and find a way to forge her own way, changed by the experience, but stronger.

Jocelyn's verbiage is laden with images, often contrasting the galactic with the visceral to riveting effect, as in the sweeping *"Blue Bird."* And at the same time, her words pay tribute and lay waste to those whom the speaker adores and yet sees for all their humanness, as in *"Meteor."* Her emotional journey is not without its humor; *"Organic Musings,"* a beautifully captured moment, leaves me with a smile. The destination of the speaker's journey climaxes beautifully in the final third of the collection, *"Body,"* in which the speaker directly addresses us, the Reader, and allows us to examine our notions of how we have chosen to love ourselves and how we have failed to love those who need it most. The final moments of the collection range from the bitterly honest (*"God's Paintbrush"*) to a solid anthem of identity in the closing poem, *"For My Body."*

Whether you have loved someone who has hurt you, or been too in love to know you were being hurt, or have realized that you have come a long way from that pain, or simply are on your own journey of self-love, however that may look, you will find a point of connection, if not several, in the careful and moving structure of *"Soul Meets Body."* We would be lying to ourselves to deny that we haven't at some point confronted our own imperfections. Jocelyn has done so, and the result of this outpouring of verbal art is a discovery of bravery. Live on and love on.

For my old friend,
Luis Antonio Gonzalez,
Playwright and Director,
Annabella the Musical.

Soul Meets Body
Table of Contents

Part 1: SOUL

Part 2: MEETS

Part 3: BODY

*"I want to live where soul meets body
and let the sun wrap its arms around me
and bathe my skin in water cool and
cleansing
and feel, feel what it's like to be new"
~Death Cab for Cutie, Soul Meets Body*

Soul

Meets

Body

By

Jocelyn Mosman

Part 1: SOUL

"Beautiful music is the art of the prophets that can calm the agitations of the soul; it is one of the most magnificent and delightful presents God has given us." ~Martin Luther

Allusions of the Soul

My soul is black as night,
crumbling like sand castles
in my cracked palms,

split like Humpty Dumpty,
dropped from the Great Wall of Heaven,
until love was more powerful than hate.

Busting open and spilling
its contents across a world of sin,
spewing my jigsaw puzzle through the night

until my eyes reflected Hitler's grey soul,
the colour of a cloudy day,
filled with more rain than the Floods.

I am trapped in the body of a child,
dancing and pirouetting around Fate,
a caged bird learning to sing,

as blind Justice misses her bull's-eye
and pins her arrow directly inside me,
like Cupid's shaft, removing love.

I feel the moon shine down.
I am warrior of life,
beating out the drums,

I hear my heart beating,
beating, beating, like a raven's wings,
a battle cry—

My world dissipates like smoke

from a candle extinguished
by acolytes as they march down the aisle.

Locked in a cage with Satan, Jesus, and Dante,
I watch the sand slip through
the empty spaces in my fingers,

and I think of you,
miles and miles away as
the tide is pulled in by Diana,

as my soul floats away,
like a red balloon,
drifting off into the black, black sky.

O, the Crimes of the Heart.

If You Were Nature

I'd dig my fingers into all of you,
let your dirt get under my fingernails,
claw my way to your surface.
Nature would spill out of your esophagus
and gush from your spread limbs.
I'd plant seeds in your abdomen,
watch stretch marks grow like stems,
and blossom your navel.
There'd be a spade in the lifelines of your palms,
and you'd excavate your veins
until they become branches.
You'd be the trunk I'd carve our romance into.
I'd gut you open, watch you bleed.
You are the only nature
my body knows how to read.
I'd dig my fingers into your gnarled flesh,
whittle out a miniature house
and call you my hollowed home.

Rewind

Time turns backwards
every second I'm with you.
Seconds with you
feel like an eternity.
I'll reflect the sunlight in
your arms
and the moonlight
from my bare chest.
We use dials
to tell the hour,
and flowers will blossom
in winter and winter will
be spring,
and my springs will recoil
to spend negative time with you.
I wish I could remember tomorrow,
but yesterday is the only
day we have left
until we rewind again.
My biological clock
is an alarm
and I have your child
and get pregnant and fall
in love all over again.
The cuckoo cries.
The last hour we are together,
and the world starts spinning
in reverse.
I want to be with you until
the Big Bang happens.
We will turn to darkness
instead of light.

Our Love Is Electric,
Even During The Storm

I want to discover electricity
in your fingertips,
fly a kite to witness your thunderstorm,
I want to be a mad scientist,
study your every inch
and watch how you light up
my universe.
I want to hold the skeleton key that fits
comfortably in your locks.
I want to squeeze myself inside
your comfort zone
and know that we are there together.
In you, there is a blue sky
full of images and
the sunrises remind me of home.
Together, we can create lightning.
We never miss a chance
of holding our hands tight
and not letting go.
Rainy days and storm clouds never
stop us from flying.
We are always trying to discover something
completely new and terrifying
and are never scared
of the electricity of chemistry
pulsing through our veins
every time we accidentally touch.

I See Heaven

You're my guardian angel.
While we are stuck on earth with calloused feet
from putting too much pressure on ourselves,
yours are creamy and smooth.
Wings let you choose to walk or fly,
to talk amidst the clouds or make them cry.
If the pearly gates are any indication,
I'd say you were a class A lifer.
My corporeal body is not made for wings,
so don't worry about the stitching.
My wings are duck feathers,
flying south for the winter.
You're my sunny skies,
my refuge in God's eyes.
I may be just a sinner,
but every time I write,
I see you.
Every time I write,
I see Heaven.

[Instrumental]

I write lullabies
on my spine,
soothing chords,
and you're
plucking at my vertebrae
like guitar strings,
humming with every stretch.
Listen to aching
sore subjects
sending a vibrato
to my neck and collarbone.
You sing my childhood
back to me,
tracing my song lyrics
with hot breath.
I want to be the bone
breaking your silence.
My body, your instrument,
strum on my heart strings,
drum on my ivories.
I write lyrics
crosshatched like score
on my shoulder blades.
The love notes on my skin
turn into
eighth notes in your throat.
I am words swallowed
into bumpy flesh,
you are music
spilling from filled lungs.
You're comfort to my body
when I'm laid out
and eyes closed.

I dream of you playing me
from my cerebral cortex
to my coccyx,
a whole range
of beautiful
erupting from
broken chords
in my curved spine.

Blue Bird

I want my heart to grow wings
like flowers grow new petals,
blossom in the sunlight,
and I want chlorophyll
to run green in my bones,
cling to my veins,
and spill out
until I can fly.

I want to be hoisted atop
broad shoulders,
climb larger boulders,
find rooftops as the next
stepping stone on the ladder
to the heavens.

I want to fly,
let my veins tie themselves
to the feathers
and reach for the sky.

I want you to carry me
like Daedalus carried his son,
until I can carry myself.
I'm not asking to be
your guardian angel,
I'm not asking to be
your eagle,
I want to be free.

The sunrise is beckoning my name,
and so is the sunset.
Stop holding me down,

stop holding me back,
stop   holding   me.

Let me reach until my feathered wings
burn into the sun.
Let me fly until my heart grows weary.
You created a compass in me,
and I always know which way is home,
but don't limit me to the horizon.

I see the stars and the moon in your eyes,
and I'll fly straight til dawn,
let my blood vessels wrap themselves
around my blue feathers
until the sky turns a different shade of blue,
isn't it strange?

I've been flying higher
than any mountain top for so long,
I've lost sight of the beauty surrounding me.
Blue oceans, blue skies, blue blood,
color blind to my own dowry,
I miss the galaxies I saw in your deep blue eyes.

There's more than this atmosphere,
and I'm Icarus after all, flying too close
to the sun, burning up my sight.
My wings grow from my heart
like petals from flowers.

Keep carrying me to rooftops at night,
and let me see the universe
in your eyes,
let me watch the pink sunrise
in your heart.

It'll fill the black holes
in mine.

Cut away the wings
from my heart,
sew them onto you,
alis volat propiis.
They were yours all along.

You were the gardener,
giving me fresh water to grow,
and nursing a sick bird back to health.
I was a blue bird,
blind to affection and love,
driven by ambition.

You were a fallen star,
a guardian angel,
and you make me whole.

Fly on your own wings,
show me a universe that
starts with the word *Love*
and ends with the word
Recklessly.

I want fly
like a blue bird in your heart,
make tiny trails as reminders,
and sing to you
miles and miles away,
you are my wings,
my veins drink in your love
like chlorophyll.

There are so many constellations
I can voyage to through
the power of
your kiss.

Meteor

Grandpa,
I have a hole in my chest
where you landed—
a man who could speak more rhymes
than anyone I'd met.
You told me I was
a star in your galaxy,
and you had me spinning
through space.
You made me a daydreamer
because I was less afraid
in the daylight
than when having night terrors
where you were only a whisper
of the man I remembered.
I remember the day it rained,
because the atmosphere went
on strike against your absence
in my life.
You were a ghostwriter
on my mother's birthday,
painting a heart in the sky
to remind her
that it could be easily torn apart
by the breeze
and she needed to be more careful
carrying it on her sleeve.
I think she buried a piece of it
under your tombstone
when your body turned to ashes,
but my mother is a gravedigger
during the holidays,
bringing back the old memories,

talking you down out of
black and white photographs.
To me, you were just
the man who loved
poetry and Charles Dickens,
but still had space
in your heart
for me.
You always encouraged me
to break through walls
with new words.
You taught me metaphor.
My heart was a meteor bursting
in slow motion
and my mother
enveloped it into her womb.
The matriarch of my earth
took in the broken shells,
collecting the ashes as keepsakes.
But I only witnessed the aftermath,
telling me that poetry
would be the only way to
wedge out the lost time.
I feel like I missed
something
Earth shattering
because you left my family
as a Pennsylvania reflection
to the storm you'd created.
I can't write enough poetry
to make your memory
more three-dimensional,
but I'm not sure I want to
because my heart is a burial ground
where I keep those I've loved and lost

and there's a tombstone
in front with your name on it.
I'm sorry I didn't get the chance
to say goodbye.

Goodbye.

Ship Souls to Starlight

Ship souls to starlight,
watch the rowing of
oars in choppy waters
crinkle the refracted moon,
crying out for peace.

Ship to starry night
the smooth stone skipping
like a gentle heartbeat
across ebbing lakes and
plopping to the bottom.

Sinking deep, sinking deeper,
until it fully drinks
moonlight into its pores.
A milky film pours
out like moonlit eyes.

Ship death to Tartarus
under care of Charon,
drowning in the moaning
of souls cut short
by winged spiteful Fates.

Ship my soul, too
and let me explore
the vast, expansive universe
as we travel together
ticking my time away.

Beyond the sweeping heavens,
above the rolling seas,
atop the palatial mountains,

between the desolate plains,
over the unbridled hills.

Let me be a
pebble in calm waters
finding the light just
below the surface of
the dark, dark unknown.

Apocalypse

I'll write sunrises
into your eyes
so I can watch a new day
growing within you.

I'll write a hundred
midnight haikus,
so you can paint battle scars,
echoing our past.

I will make two rose beds,
and garden your cheeks
to bloom tender,
despite the scratches.

I will reach my hand
out as far as it can go,
so I will forever be
reaching for your touch.

My fingers turn into powder
when I look into your
apocalyptic
soul.

Part 2: MEETS

"I like a man with a flexible mind, you said then,
lifting your candlelit glass to me
and I raised mine to you and began to wonder
what life would be like as one of your ribs—"
~Billy Collins, Genesis

Soul Meets Body

My body is a glass house:
easily broken and raw,
I teach myself how to be
more than my imprisoning flesh.
I am
arteries and veins
heart and love
bleeding.
I belong
where soul meets body.
I belong,
bleeding,
heart and love,
arteries and veins.
I am
more than my imprisoning flesh.
I teach myself how to be
easily broken and raw:
my body is a glass house.

God's Paintbrush

I am sitting at a coffee shop,
reading poetry.
You walk in
with a new partner
and pretend you don't see me.

Your head bent over,
hers on your shoulder,
hands intertwining
like colors run together,
like God had a paintbrush
and was creating the masterpiece
of screw you's to my love life.

From here I can see
your lungs working
overtime to keep
your breathing controlled,
the rise and fall of each rib,
like Rome was built
on top of your
promises.

I'm sitting behind you,
glaring.
Your body never
fails you,
steadfast, like you have
an addiction
to looking straight ahead.

Splotches of red
soak your face,

like God created war paint
for all the battles you fought
to get here.

I remember our hands,
clasping,
our palms outstretched
with lifelines touching.
We were never meant
to have our futures read.

I can't be brought back
to the origins
of who we were.
When you first looked
at me...
you in a Spider-Man mask...
dragging me into Bath and Body Works...
kissing me and kissing me until
I couldn't see...

Rating our sex life on a scale
of 1 to 10...
telling me to choose
between college and you...
two years of radio silence...
an affair...
Oh, how I used to believe you...

You and those freckles,
that face, that smile,
that ugly jacket...
You ruined my one attempt
at a love life.

My love life?
Two broken pieces of asphalt
disintegrating from under me.

Can you not hear me crumble,
or are you ignoring my collapse?

Playing Love

we played house, but never home for a year of
unorthodox loving our relationship was car rides
in broken down jeeps with duct taped windows
shopping cart romances in the yogurt aisle
stealing bacon at the local cracker barrel

we played mommy and daddy to your two dogs
but their real mommy was daddys ex wife split
custody of dogs and clothing i felt like the other
woman exiled from the eden of our love affair

we played king and queen without the royalty
sprawled across your bed like a housewife we
created fortresses out of the sheets to block out
the world around us we were stolen glances in
classes quiet kisses in an empty parking lot

we never played teacher and student it felt too
much like reality in the fiction we wanted to
create from our story the quiet never felt more
like torture than the moments of silence in
shared spaces where fingers intertwined like
butterflies and ribbons

we played adam and eve wearing only each
others kiss as clothing until the shame of our
sinful nature set in god promised us fruit but my
barren soil told us even eden could not last
forever

we played house for a year but never did our
hearts resonate the sound of forever home i was

just a squatter for a while but we never could
have made it to til death do us part

we were playing into the fiction of an impossible
and unorthodox love

Eulogy for a Muffin

It was a good muffin,
the way it crumbled gently
as it touched my moist lips.
It knew no other mouth but mine.
It was made with care
and dedication and love,
baked from some kitchen.
I don't know who baked it,
but I like to pretend it was
a big burly man with a beard.
Something about this muffin,
it tasted like strength,
had the consistency
of my father's belt,
and taught me patience
as it melted on my tongue.
A beautiful muffin!
Its aroma filled the entire room,
smelling of sweet pumpkin
and spice and all things
naughty and nice.
It reminded me of Christmas-
the one we had at my Grandma's
in Pennsylvania
after Grandpa died.
It was sweet,
but had just a hint of salt.
I can't be sure if the baker
cried when mixing ingredients,
if he, too, had felt loss.
This muffin left its remains sticky
on my fingers
like ashes,

like play dough,
like muffin dough
if muffins are made
using dough.
(I'm not sure, I don't cook.)
I wanted to know
the man behind this muffin,
the great bearded one.
I wanted to meet the two cats,
calico and black,
that crawled up onto the counter,
blocking the view of
the recipe,
and made this man create
this muffin
literally by scratch.
I wanted to know this muffin man,
the one who lives on Drury Lane.
He created a muffin so insatiable,
metaphors won't do it justice.
A muffin like that would win
poetry slams
because it was so poetic
when devoured,
and the empty plate,
licked clean by two cats,
calico and black,
looked more like a broken heart
than a well-loved dish.
The plate and me,
me and the plate,
we tasted the tears
of the man behind this muffin.
We both knew tonight,
there would be

no more
inspirational muffins
to kiss us goodnight.

Rooted

I.

You are rhythm turning words
into music and music
into air and air into lungs.
You are each vertebrae standing
straight and tall,
each lump in the throat
swallowing back pain for pride.

II.

You are still so young at heart,
but an old soul.
You speak trees
into existence,
climb on nothing until
branches appear beneath you.
You spoke me
into existence, too.

III.

You remind me that space
is key to understanding,
but I don't understand.
When your body attacks
itself from the inside,
you are silent.
You   leave   space.

IV.

You remind me that
comedy is tragedy plus time.
Your pain, reflected
will always be
tragic, no matter how much
time passes.

V.

When everyone else faded,
you stood and listened;
against a tilted world,
you did not abandon me.
When canyons formed,
you showed me freedom.

VI.

You speak
trees into existence,
make spiritual connections
with roots and trunk and leaves.
I am not a tree to be spoken into,
but my heart is gnarly and
I can give you
                    space.

i need

the spirituality of skin;

joy
in flesh and bone
and all ten thousand emotions;

pain
that brings consciousness;

that ridiculous smile;

a grandiose chuckle;

chocolate or your eyes
or both;

a spine
to support yours
like a double helix;

a life vest;

a titanic heart
when i'm drowning
and there is no land in sight;

a lighthouse calling me home;

sand like time spilling out;

the wrinkled shoreline of neck;

to be able to say

the words caught in
my fishnet throat:

i. love. you.

In The Beginning

I like to imagine at night,
when the sky is speckled
with stars and each looks
like a different freckle on
your sleeping face,
that I was made from
your rib.

I am attached to your backbone,
giving you strength and support
whether you know it or not...

I am attached to your sternum,
curving around your organs,
like ebony and ivory keys
in a consecrated chapel,
resonating with every twist and turn
of your torso.

I am the protector of your heart,
pumping life just beneath
your chest.

I am the protector of your lungs,
aware of your constant breath,
unfailing as it travels from day
to night to day.

As you arch your back
to make love to me,
I cannot help but notice
how thin you look,
how your ribs protrude

from your skin
like a lost dog.

I want to be the meat
on your bones,
the delicious bits
you savor like memories.

I lean my head against
your ribs and count them,
as I count my blessings
to fall asleep.

Organic Musings

You say I am really cheesy,
and I ask you,
what kind?
Am I holy like Swiss,
or sharp-witted like Cheddar,
or do I grate on your nerves
like Mozzarella?

You cringe.
I laugh.

I say you are fruitful,
and you ask me,
what kind?
Are you fresh like a strawberry,
or sour like a lemon,
or tart like a blueberry?

We both laugh,
and cringe.

You are a blueberry, I say,
and I picked you.

Your eyes match the night sky,
just as it reaches dusk.
If I were an artist,
I would paint your eyes
and the sky
with blueberries,
but you know I'm not.

Instead, I write poems,

and you decide
I am a little more
Mozzarella than Swiss.

We both fall asleep,
laughing.

Your Name

Your name is not poetry,
but it reminds me of you.
You are a half-shaken snow globe,
scattering cold, empty stares
on everyone close by.
You shed your emotions
like snakes shed their skin.
You are a thousand white horses
drumming their hooves
into your muddy footprints.
I wonder what future generations
will see when they examine
your remains like artifacts
and dinosaur bones.
You are a single sunflower,
painfully beautiful and sad
soaking up light after darkness.
You are science and math.
You can comprehend numbers
and molecules.
You carry yourself like a sestina,
repeating the same six words
in patterns that twist their meaning.
I am your pattern.
I am your paisley and your flannel.
I am your bad habits.
But you must be poetry because
no matter what I am to you,
you will always be guilt
and regret and empty canvas
to me.
You will be tormentor
and muse until I write

the poem that can bring you
back.
No poem will ever bring you back,
so I write love letters
on my palms with hope
one day you can hide
the scribbled words
with open hands.
You are missed opportunity
and almost love.
Our past is millions
of miles of unresolved emotions.
You are a lighthouse
in the distance
beckoning me back to you.
You are my lucid images at 3 am.
You will never come true.
But I'll keep whispering
your name into my pillow
and wishing on you instead
of candles and shooting stars.
Your name may not be poetry,
but it sure as hell reminds me
of you.

Universe Body

1. The back of my hand is a universe. I keep an entire galaxy of freckles there. I name my blemishes after planets, moons, and supernovas. It's alien to your telescopic eyes.

2. My wrist is a rainbow. I've been following the black, blue, red, and yellow curve to find a pot of gold. You dig below to bury the treasure inside me.

3. My arm is a tree branch. I tried to carve forgiveness into it, but forever is a long time for you to stay, swinging.

4. My shoulder blade is a chalkboard. I hoped for a blank slate. You dig your nails into me. I fit nicely in your trophy case.

5. My neck is a lemon. You pucker up at the taste, put salt on the wound, and bite. Our bittersweet romance.

Part 3: BODY

"If you look closely at a tree, you'll notice its knots and dead branches, just like our bodies. What we learn is that beauty and imperfection go together wonderfully." ~Matthew Fox

How to Love a Fat Girl

She's beautiful,
and everything I never could have imagined.

She's 23 and drinking whiskey
before bedtime.
She said her dreams tasted better
when she drank.

Her hair was dyed a shade of red
and brown and black
because rainbows are for
promises, she said.
"God wouldn't lie."

She was 200 pounds
and curvy.

Her waistline was not large enough
to hold her heart,
but it was too large
to fit in a rectangular mirror.

She did not care about fitting
into mirrors or boxes or bra sizes.

She said it felt better when she
left her clothes in the drawers
and just walked around
feeling her skin connect with nature.

When I wanted to have sex with her,
she asked me, "Screw or make love?
There is a difference."

She did not turn off the light
to get undressed.

She's the most beautiful woman
I have ever witnessed.

Tattoos were strewn across her body
like the Sistine Chapel.
I'd never seen art look so holy.

She took my hand and placed it
just above her heart.
She told me that it beat a little faster
because she might be slightly
out of shape.

I told her that I loved her shape.
She laughed.

"Nobody loves a fat girl," she said.
"Women like us are supposed to
fall in love with people like you."
She said. "We are supposed to fall,
and we are supposed to stay down."

She's the most beautiful woman
I have ever met and yet she swore
that I did not love her.

She swore that
I did not see her face turn pale
when she stepped onto a scale
or in front of a mirror.

I told her that I know
I did not see her pain and
I did not see her past.
I just saw a beautiful woman.

I told her
that's all I needed to see
to know how to love her.

Fragile Women

Our slit wrists are
severe weather alerts,
and we are sounding out
unnatural disasters.
We bleed until our palms
are clasped together
dripping our prayers
onto cracked canvases.
We keep
our hearts like angel wings,
growing a feather with every
heartbreak,
and I know women
who are flying right now.
They bleed out too many
days without sunrises
keep tally marks
on their flesh,
wait for their chance
to breathe again
without having to bite their tongues,
and swallow
bloody saliva
that tastes like their unspoken self-defenses.
I know women whose DNA
turned against them,
created a pallet of brown
and grey and emptiness,
never satisfied with their
shade of pretty.
I know women whose
hearts are breaking
without the metaphor.

They are pleading
without any god
for a new one before
theirs erupted in the ER...
2015 has a way of breaking
women's hearts,
and teenage girls are bleeding out
broken futures.
I know women who are performing
exorcisms on their spirits,
hoping that their unholy ghost
paints their wings white
with every slice of the knife.
Fragile women,
bodies made beautiful,
and self-destructive.
We aren't meant to bleed
like martyrs.
Don't cast down your faces,
look into the places
of your body
you've never seen.
Every hair is a part of your halo,
every scar is a rose petal
for you to garden
with self-love.
Fragile women,
we are born to be strong,
ashes being relit
into the fire
we started from.
Let our bruises become candles
guiding our angels with broken wings
and misplaced spirits
home.

Reliance

You are every stretch of tendon,
wrist flexed, then relaxed,
the curvature of hand,
steady and bent.

You are brain stem activity,
words and pain both flowing
down your spinal cord
until it is too hard to write.

You are mouth and throat,
soft spoken and fragile,
swallowing blood,
choking back heart.

You rely on the body:
hand to write,
spine to stand,
mouth to speak.

As you collapse inward
like a burning house,
all I can do is hold sound
the walls,

resist the destruction,
or flee.

I will not leave.
I will not watch you burn.

I will guide your hand,
until words flow past

unspeakable pain
onto open page.

I will stand tall beside you,
become sturdy,
lumbar vertebrae,
help you climb and stretch.

I will give your voice legacy,
as student, as friend,
next generation of oral tradition
passed hand-to-hand like communion,

but when the house smolders,
the skeleton screams,
the joints crack.
I smell smoke.

As body relies on body,
I rely on you.

I will not leave.
I will not watch you burn.

Poetry in Fragments

I.
Your poetry reminds me
of my past.
Last year is the rear view mirror
of your backwards words.

II.
Your lips are cigarette smoke
and ashy rings.
I gave up
the only life I knew
just to be with you.

III.
Your body is
mountains and valleys.
I know where you excavated
your insides
to find remains of former lovers.

IV.
Your eyes are chiseled
from marble.
You ooze
more pseudo-affection
than anyone I've ever met.

V.
Your heart is a cave
of ventricles and aorta.
I want to go spelunking to find
the corners of your ribcage.

VI.
Your backwards words
are the rear view mirror
of last year.
The past reminds me
of your poetry.

Ten Lies I Wrote About Us

I never loved you.
My heart doesn't ache when I hear your name.
I don't ever secretly stalk your Facebook
account.
In fact, I don't even miss you.
When you left me, I was happy.
When you left me, every cell in my body relaxed.
I never eat my feelings.
My feelings never taste like chocolate.
Chocolate makes up for you leaving.
You leaving is the best thing that ever happened
to me.

Wrestling Match

Round 1:

It came to you in a dream
and you never questioned
God's plan to name me Jocelyn.

Champion.
There was no doubt
I would grow up a fighter.

Round 2:

You gave me ambition,
but called it passion.
I was to be a lawyer, you said.

It was perfect for your daughter
who loved to argue.
It was perfect. I wasn't.

We wrestled our way through long disputes.
We held our ground,
despite the pain.

Round 3:

Every time I fell down,
you picked me up.
Keep fighting. Bruises fade.

You faded when I moved north,
and my heart was too heavy
a suitcase to unpack.

Round 4:

If you peeled back the tough love
and admitted you were proud
of the woman I had become,

you'd notice my battle cry,
you'd listen to my barbaric yawp, exalted.
you'd hear my tribal chant, victorious.

Round 5:

My sins look like yours
when you tuck them in at night.
I have your temper and your rage.

Now, we wrestle our way through silence.
We still hold our ground,
despite the pain.

Love me, human.
Neither of us looks holy
when morning comes.

Black Dress And Combat Boots

She wore a black dress
and combat boots.

She said she felt ready
for whatever battle came her way.

Her boots were for fighting, she said.
She had taken enough self-defense
to understand how to kick
and how to punch.

She wore a black dress
and combat boots.

Surprise panic attacks left her
shaking before public speaking.
She was not ready to tell
the world the truth.

Her clothing was her only weapon
against the enemy lines
chalking out her silhouette
on the sidewalk.

She saw shadows around every corner
and on the edges of her peripheral vision.
She swore the world was against her.

She wore a black dress
and combat boots.

She wore them because she knew
how it felt to be fighting against society.

She wore them as a uniform.
She said, "I've always been at war
with myself and the mirror."

She wore a black dress
and combat boots,

because she was prepared
to stay on this side
of heaven for another day.

Neurosis

I am dark matter, white noise.
I can't fall asleep
in midnight's unrelenting
        stillness.

The quiet makes
everyone and everything outside
disappear and
        I feel alone.

I don't know how to be alone
without losing my self.
Anxiety sets in
        like mist.

I evade shadows,
lose focus as the sun
rises and
        sets.

Some days,
I can't keep up.
I need to breathe
        but I can't.

I am trapped
on this blue planet,
silently spinning
        through space.

The world I was born into was
a muted scream made audible
in the emergency exit

of my mother's belly.

I have made 21 revolutions
around a sun
I cannot control,
        a cycling of

waves, planets, bicycles, periods,
This noisy rhythm is dull
against my
        heartbeat.

The compression of blood
in and out of ventricles
in and out of veins,
        out of me:

like the ocean
washing the beach
after footprints litter
        its pristine shoreline;

like the final squeeze
of catsup before it reaches
its sputtering and anticlimactic
        finish;

like you
sighing, begging me
to stop being
        so neurotic.

Each year, a twister
that sweeps me off my feet
day after day, but I always find

my way home.

I don't know where home is,
not anymore,
but being here with you
        seems right.

The snow is silent as dots
falling from the darkness
of the heavens
        onto spindly trees

The world is quiet here,
except the wind
on the window pane,
        and you beside me.

You hold my hand,
our body heat colliding
in the darkness and
        I can't let go.

Short Girl

I've always been known as
       the short girl.
Never able to reach the top shelf
       short girl.
Have trouble kissing tall guys
       short girl.
"Would you like a kids menu?"
       short girl.
I've heard every possible
joke regarding my height.
I've been called:
       fun size,
       shorty,
       leprechaun,
       bite size,
       dwarf,
       shortstop,
       half pint,
       peanut
       munchkin,
       midget,
       small fry,
       tater tot,
       shrimp,
       short stack,
       and little woman.
The best thing I've ever heard was
       "one small step for man,
       one giant leap for Jocelyn."
I found it hilarious at the time,
and some days I still do,
but when being short
made bullying easier,

it didn't seem as funny.
When a boy could hold
my possessions above my head,
make me jump for it,
and never quite reach,
I felt the gravity of patriarchy
weighing me down.
My doctor told me
I was supposed to be 5'8,
but my growing stopped
in the fifth grade,
my bones hardened,
and my height is
stuck at 4'11 (and three-quarters).
I'm the less-than-5'-
lied-about-my-height-
on-my-driver's-license-
limbo-champion-
for-the-last-several-rounds
       short girl.
I'm not saying that being short
doesn't have its benefits.
I can sneak through a crowd
of people without being noticed,
but I never get to see the singers
at a concert or the actors onstage
if a tall man decides to plant
himself in front of me.
(He always plants himself
in front of me!)
I know that being short
means being seen as less of a person.
That I'm only half of what others are,
but being short doesn't make me
inferior or unimportant.

It just means that I need
a smaller microphone
or a large pedestal to stand on.
And when it's raining outside,
maybe the storm will be over
when it reaches my head.
After all,
I'm not just
            the short girl.
I'm an anatomically compact
and phenomenally beautiful woman.
I'm more than my height.
I'm more than my size 3 shoes.
I'm more than my size youth gloves.
I'm more than my inadequacies.
To you, I may be
            the short girl,
but when I climb up onto
the kitchen counter
in my secret-ninja-gymnast-like ways
to reach the glass on the top shelf,
I will always be cooler than you!
It may be a small step
for man,
but it is a quick run,
a giant leap,
a sprint forward
for me.
And I will always work
twice as hard to be
the woman I want to be
because it isn't easy
being stared at.
or laughed at.
I just have to pretend

that God knew all along
not to make me tall.
The higher you are,
the further you fall,
and I have a fear of heights.

For My Body

For my big bones, short torso, and small feet.
For my stretch marks and my scars,
my icy skin and burning blood.
For every curly strand of hair
and every freckle.

For my dry skin.
For my pimples that arise one week
every month,
like a Brigadoon of pimples.
For baby fat I never
grew into or outgrew.

For womanhood that churns
like butter.
For these breasts I inherited
from my grandmother.
For my pelvis made wide
to birth new life.
For my womb that may
never hold a child,
my genes that may never
be called Mom.

For my iron deficient blood,
for my migraines,
oh god, for my migraines!
For taking migraine medication every night.

For the hair follicles
digging deep into my brain,
like words not yet discovered.
For the discovery of electricity,

in the waves of kinetic energy
sent to my fingers.

My stubby fingertips.
(For those, too).
For these hands that hold
my niece's baby fingers one day
and a pocket knife the next.

For this body I love in,
emotions tangling like spaghetti
and curly hair
and a heart
always off-beat.
For my veins like lightning-struck branches,
for my spine like a redwood tree,
for when I am most bare.

For the scars on my elbows
from falling off the jungle gym.
For the discoloration on my kneecaps
from tripping up stairs.
For my trembling ankles...

For the zigzags on my belly
from three operations.
For the abscess in my uterus
the doctor forgot when stitching
me up.
For my appendix that burst
at the Harry Potter midnight premier.

For my hourglass figure
running out of time,
for never having enough,

always having too much.
For never quite fitting no matter
how much I squeeze and pull
and don't breathe.

For wanting
to be less curvy.
For wishing for smaller hips.
For wishing plus size and thighs
didn't rhyme so well.
For wanting a body tailored
to me.
For trying to be someone else.

For still never fitting.
For knowing I am not perfect.
For that being okay.
For forgiveness.
For this body I live in.

Epilogue

Jocelyn Mosman

About the author

Jocelyn Mosman is twenty-one years old, and a student at Mount Holyoke College. She is double majoring in English and Politics, with concentrations in poetry and international law.

This is Mosman's third poetry book, following Soul Music (2013) and Soul Painting (2014). Mosman has also been published in a variety of anthologies, literary journals, and magazines.

She recently received poetry awards for her work at Mount Holyoke and outside. She is active in poetry slams in Northampton, MA, along with being part of multiple poetry societies in both Texas and Massachusetts. She was also a member of the first ever Northampton Poetry Slam Team (2015).

She is the founder of the West Texas Poets, the former president of the Permian Basin Chapter, Poetry Society of Texas, a regular of Northampton Poetry, and a board member of the Conscious Poets Society.

She has opened for Mary Lambert, Beau Sia, Mayda del Valle, Jesse Parent, Buddy Wakefield, Striver's Row, Shira Erlichman, Anthony Anaxagorou, Sally Jenkinson, and more.

Acknowledgments

Grateful acknowledgment is made to the following journals and anthologies, in which these poems originally appeared, sometimes in slightly different form.

If You Were Nature: Red Fez
Rewind: VerseWrights
Our Love Is Electric, Even During The Storm: Inner Child Press
I See Heaven: Red Fez, The Wait Anthology
[Instrumental]: Rogue Particles Magazine
Blue Bird: This Time Around: Passport, Teen Ink, Inner Child Press, Cum Laude Weekly
Meteor: Teen Ink, Inner Child Press
Ship Souls to Starlight: The Merrimack Review
Apocalypse: Black Mirror Magazine
Soul Meets Body: WNQ Writers, Black Mirror Magazine
God's Paintbrush: Snapping Twig, Cultured Vultures
Playing Love: Yellow Chair Review, Snapping Twig
Eulogy for a Muffin: Dead Snakes, Bitchin' Kitsch
Rooted: Tuck Magazine, Snapping Twig
i need: VerseWrights, Piker Press
In The Beginning: Kool Kids Press, Eunoia Review, Piker Press
Organic Musings: Kool Kids Press
Your Name: Academy of American Poets
Universe Body: Harbinger Asylum
How To Love A Fat Girl: Rogue Particles Magazine, The Unrorean, Inner Child Press, VerseWrights , The Fat Damsel
Fragile Women: Red Fez, West Texas Poets, Drunk Monkeys, Stop the Beauty Madness, Inner Child Press, I Am Not A Silent Poet, VerseWrights, Northampton Poetry
Reliance: Yellow Chair Review, Tuck Magazine, Poems and Poetry, Leaves of Ink, Piker Press, Snapping Twig, Peeking Cat
Ten Lies I Wrote About Us: Rogue Particles Magazine, Black Mirror Magazine
Wrestling Match: Yellow Chair Review, Silver Birch Press
Black Dress and Combat Boots: Your One Phone Call
Neurosis: VerseWrights, Indiana Voice Journal, Snapping Twig, Carcinogenic Poetry, Virgogray Press
Short Girl: Northampton Poetry
For My Body: WNQ Writers, I Am Not a Silent Poet, Kool Kids Press, Academy of American Poets, Northampton Poetry

Special Thanks

To Northampton Poetry, West Texas Poets, Conscious Poets Society, Word Out, and my extended poetry family, without you, I would be a lost voice echoing into the silence.

To Craig Nelson, Robert Shaw, and Jelene Ballard, I could not ask for better guidance.

To Whisky and Beards Publishing for their undying support in making this book a reality.

To my family, poetic or otherwise, thank you for sticking with me and being part of my life.

To my friends, poetic or otherwise, thank you for loving a poet because of who I am, not despite it.

To Luis Antonio Gonzalez, thank you for your friendship over the years and your kind words.

To Sarah Frances Moran, thank you for your ongoing support and mutual admiration.

To my muses, these poems would not exist without you.

Web Links

Facebook
www.facebook.com/JocelynMosman

Twitter
www.twitter.com/JocelynMosman

Email
jmosman7@aol.com

Website
mosma22j.wix.com/jocelynmosman

Made in the USA
Middletown, DE
09 January 2016